What Instrument Is This ?

Rosmarie Hausherr

 SCHOLASTIC INC.   New York

Acknowledgments

I would like to thank all the children who were photographed for this book, and the parents for their patience and help. It was a special pleasure to be working with professional musicians who generously offered time and information. A big thank you to the numerous music teachers for sharing their professional experiences and their enthusiasm. I am thankful for the generous support from: The Third Street Music School Settlement, NYC; The Harlem School of the Arts, NYC; The Swiss Institute, NYC; Joffrey Ballet School, NYC; The Julliard School/Harp Department, NYC; CBGB, NYC; The Peacham Library, VT; and Johnathan Strasser, conductor, NYC. A warm thank you to Carol and Ethan Marunas; the Magnus family; Felix Wey; and to the many friends who helped with instruments, props, photography, and valuable networking. I am grateful to my editor, Dianne Hess, for her clear vision on this project; to Claire Counihan, art director, for her technical expertise; and to Anthony Kramer for his charming illustrations. Thank you, Inge Heide Druckrey, for the beautiful book design.

Words that are in *italic* in the text are explained in the glossary on page 36.

Dedication

This book is dedicated to my parents, whose love for classical music enriched my life from early childhood on. My mother, Margrith Hausherr, a devoted violin player, was a member of several orchestras for over fifty years. My father, Paul Hausherr, played the viola. At retirement age, he founded a symphony orchestra for senior citizens in Lucerne, Switzerland. Their photograph appears on the title page.

Rosmarie Hausherr

Library of Congress Cataloging-in-Publication Data

Hausherr, Rosmarie.
    What instrument is this? / Rosmarie Hausherr.
        p.   cm.
        Summary: Identifies an array of popular musical instruments and discusses how they are made, how they sound, and the styles of music for which they are best suited.
    ISBN 0-590-44644-4
    1. Musical instruments—Juvenile literature. (1. Musical instruments.) I. Title.
    ML460.H37 1992
    784.19—dc20

                                              91-19297
                                          784.19—dc20
                                                  CIP
                                               AC MN

12 11 10 9 8 7 6 5 4 3 2 1   2 3 4 5 6 7/9
Printed in the United States of America   36
First Scholastic printing, November 1992

What instrument is a long, hollow piece of wood with eight holes?

Wind Instrument:
Woodwind

The RECORDER is a favorite instrument among children.
It is easy to play and light to carry.

When a musician blows into the whistle mouthpiece with
the holes uncovered, air vibrates with a shrill, high *note*.

As the holes are covered with the tips of the fingers, the
notes become lower and lower. This is called fingering.

The recorder's music has a warm and cheerful sound.

What instrument is played sideways and can sing like a bird?

Wind Instrument:
Woodwind

Like the recorder, the FLUTE is a *pipe* with sounds that change by covering and uncovering holes. But instead of fingertips, *keyhole covers* open and close the holes.

Thousands of years ago, flutes were made of hollow animal bones, and later carved from wood. They are still called woodwinds, even though today they are made of silver, gold, and other metals.

What instrument is long and black and has keys, rings, and rods?

Wind Instrument:
Woodwind

The CLARINET is a black, wooden tube with a flared bell.

The musician fingers the notes by pressing the shiny keys, rings, and rods that open and close the holes. A small piece of *reed* (sliced from cane — a tall, dry grass) is fastened to the mouthpiece. As the clarinetist blows into the mouthpiece, the reed vibrates, producing a rich, velvety sound.

What instrument is a long, bent horn loaded with shiny keyhole covers?

Wind Instrument:
Woodwind

The SAXOPHONE, which was invented by Adolph Sax, is made of shiny brass. Because the sound is made by a single reed vibrating against a mouthpiece like the clarinet, it belongs to the woodwind family.

Fingering the keyhole covers is easier than it looks. With high notes at the top and low notes at the bottom, *octaves* are simply switched with the octave key.

Vibrant, throaty saxophones are the soul of jazz.

What instrument is played through a bag filled with air?

Wind Instrument:
Woodwind

The BAGPIPE is an ancient woodwind from the British Isles.

The piper blows lots of air into the bag through the blowpipe. The left arm presses air from the bag into three reed pipes at the top *(drones)*, which have a fixed "whining" sound. The reed pipe at the bottom *(chanter)* is fingered like a recorder and plays the *melody*.

On St. Patrick's Day the bagpiper's tune echoes in the streets with haunting magic.

What instrument makes you think of kings and queens?

Wind Instrument:
Brass

The festive, regal-sounding TRUMPET is a long, thin horn that is bent into a "paper clip" shape.

The musician puckers his lips, then blows air into a round mouthpiece, producing the sound from his buzzing lips. The trumpet's three *valves* play the notes by blocking or passing air. When placed in the bell of the trumpet, a plastic cup *(mute)* can soften the trumpet's loud voice to sound as if it's coming from far away.

What instrument looks like a shiny boa constrictor with a wide-open mouth?

Wind Instrument:
Brass

The SOUSAPHONE, the giant-sized tuba, was named for its inventor, the American composer John Philip Sousa.

The forty-pound instrument wraps around the musician, who carries much of its weight on the left shoulder. Like the trumpet, it has three valves and a round mouthpiece and is played the same way.

Because of the sousaphone's size, it takes enormous lung power to produce its thunderous sounds.

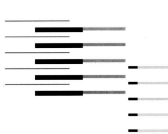
What instrument is played tucked between the chin and the left shoulder?

Strings

The VIOLIN (also called a "fiddle") is a hollow wooden box with an elegant neck and four strings.

The violinist's right hand glides or bounces a *bow* made of horsehair across the strings to produce the sound. Notes are played by pressing one or more strings against the violin's neck with the left fingers.

The violin's rich, melodic voice makes it the most important instrument in the orchestra. It also is very popular for fiddling music for bluegrass and square dances.

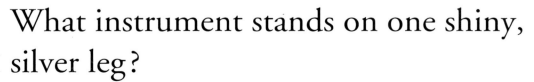 What instrument stands on one shiny, silver leg?

Strings

The beautifully shaped CELLO looks like a large violin. But its voice is deeper and richer.

The cellist sits, secures the instrument between both knees, and leans it against her chest. Notes are fingered and bowed as on the violin. But the musician's left-hand fingers have twice as far to stretch.

Cellos make beautiful music when played alone or with other instruments.

What is the most popular instrument?

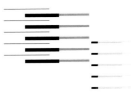

Strings

Long ago, the ACOUSTIC GUITAR was brought across the ocean to us from Spain.

The shapely wooden instrument sits in the musician's lap or hangs from a shoulder strap. Guitarists strum or pluck the six nylon or metal strings with one hand. The other hand changes notes by pressing the strings against the fingerboard.

Folk, classical, and intriguing Spanish music all come to life on the guitar.

What instrument is played by rock stars?

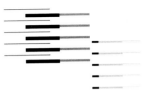

Strings

The slim-bodied ELECTRIC GUITAR is surprisingly heavy.

Without electricity, only faint sounds can be heard when the strings are picked. But turn it on, and its music can become very loud. Tiny microphones and magnets called pick-ups are located under the strings. They magnify the sounds through the *amplifiers.*

With their electronic equipment, pop and rock guitar musicians can create wild, far-out sounds.

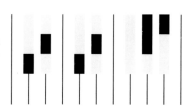 What instrument has eighty-eight black and white keys?

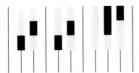

Keyboard

The full name of the PIANO is pianoforte ("piano" means soft, "forte" means loud).

When the musician's finger strikes a *key*, a small, felt-tipped hammer hits a tight, steel string inside the body to create a *tone*. The black and white keys provide seven octaves of ready-made tones. The pianist can play *chords* and melodies with both hands. The foot pedals can make tones quiet, or long-lasting. The piano can be played by two musicians sitting side by side.

 What instrument can sound like a whole orchestra?

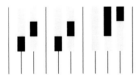

Keyboard

The PIPE ORGAN is a majestic instrument. It has two or more keyboards for the hands, and one for the feet. It also has hundreds of pipes.

As the musician plays, air flows into the many metal pipes. By pulling a knob *(stop)*, the organ can be made to sound like trumpets, flutes, strings, or even human voices.

This magnificent instrument plays powerful music in large churches and concert halls.

 What instruments are beaten with sticks and brushes?

Percussion

DRUMS and CYMBALS are a group of *rhythm* instruments, played by one musician. A drum is a round tube with a skin stretched across it. The pitch varies with size and tightness of the *drumhead*. Cymbals are thin, flat brass disks that are loosely fastened to metal stands.

Drummers use a wide variety of wooden sticks and metal brushes for different sound effects. From its hard-driving rock beat to its lyrical jazz rhythms, the drum is the pulse of the music.

 What instrument is a drum that jingles?

Percussion

The TAMBOURINE is a round frame with skin stretched over it. There are loose metal discs around the sides.

Musicians hold this small percussion instrument with one hand. They shake it, hit it, rap it, or tap it. But no one can play a melody on a tambourine.

 What instrument has bars that are not chocolate?

The hardwood bars of the XYLOPHONE ring when they are tapped with a mallet. Mallets are sticks with rubber-ball tips.

A musician strikes the short bars for high notes, and hits the longer bars for lower notes. Metal tubes below each of the wooden bars resonate the bright, bell-like sound.

In the hands of a skilled xylophonist, as many as six mallets may dance up and down the four octaves.

What instrument do we all have from the moment we are born?

Voice

The human VOICE is the most precious instrument.

Voices have *pitch*. They can sound happy or sad. They can sound loud or soft. They can make melodies and rhythms. No two voices sound alike. Women's voices are higher than men's. Young boys' voices become deeper in their early teens.

Singing voices touch our feelings with their beautiful sounds and words.

More Musical Instruments

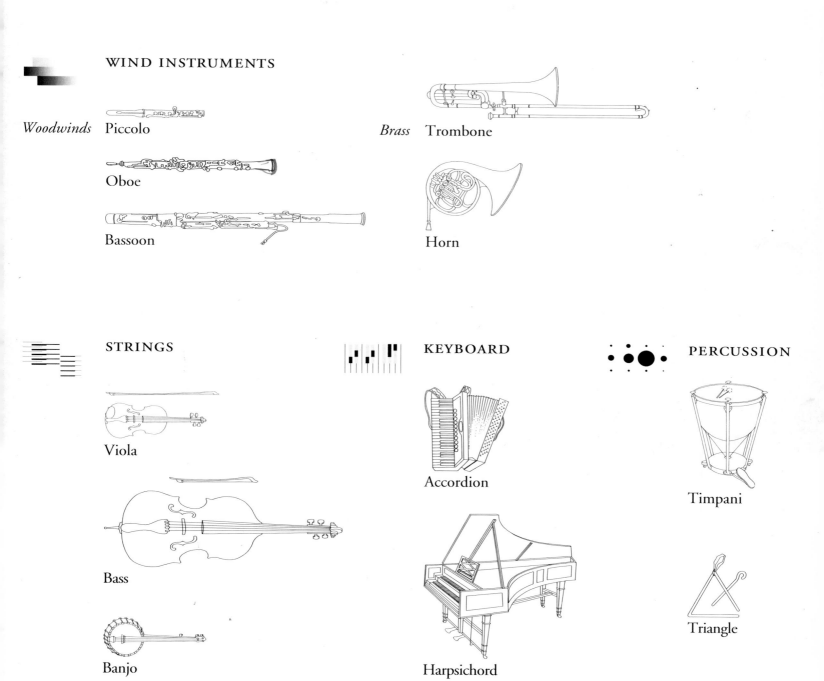

WIND INSTRUMENTS

Woodwinds Piccolo

Oboe

Bassoon

Brass Trombone

Horn

STRINGS

Viola

Bass

Banjo

KEYBOARD

Accordion

Harpsichord

PERCUSSION

Timpani

Triangle

The Four Instrument Groups

WIND INSTRUMENTS

These are musical instruments in which the player blows to produce the sound. There are two categories. Woodwinds are usually made of wood, and often have reeds attached to the mouthpiece. Brass instruments are made of metal.

STRING INSTRUMENTS

These are usually hollow wooden boxes or frames with any number of strings tightly stretched over them. They are played with a bow or plucked with the fingers.

KEYBOARD INSTRUMENTS

These have one or more rows of black and white keys. On some, when a key is pressed down, a string is struck or plucked to produce a tone. On others, an air valve is opened into a pipe that makes a sound inside the hollow space.

PERCUSSION INSTRUMENTS

These are the instruments that are struck by the musician with a hand or beaten with sticks, mallets, or brushes to produce a rhythmic sound. Some percussion instruments are made of metal, like cymbals or the triangle. Others are hollow cylinders with skins stretched tightly over them. Some are made of wood like the xylophone.

Glossary

Amplifier: A piece of electrical equipment that can make sounds louder.

Bow: A rod with long hairs from a horse's tail stretched tightly from one end to the other. The bow creates the sounds in violins and instruments of the viol families by being pulled across the strings.

Chanter: The reed pipe at the bottom of a bagpipe that plays the melody and is fingered like a recorder.

Chords: A combination of tones played at the same time.

Drone: Any of the three reed pipes at the top of a bagpipe that produces a fixed "whining" sound.

Drumhead: The skin stretched over the open end of a drum.

Key: The rectangle wooden, ivory, or plastic lever on a keyboard instrument that is pressed to set off the mechanism that produces the sound.

Keyhole cover: A flat disc that covers a sound hole on a wind instrument to create a tone.

Melody: A combination of tones played or sung in sequence that sound pleasant together; the tune of a song.

Mute: A device for softening or muffling the sound of a musical instrument.

Note: The written symbol for each sound. A musical tone.

Octave: Octo means "eight" in Latin. There are eight tones in a scale. The eighth tone is one octave higher than the first one.

Pipe: A hollow metal or wooden tube.

Pitch: The sound of one musical tone on a tonal scale.

Reed: A thin slice of a cane (a tall, dry grass) that vibrates to create the sound in some woodwinds.

Stop: A knob or pull that regulates the pipes in an organ to imitate sounds of different instruments.

Rhythm: A beat with a pattern.

Tone: A sound with a definite pitch.

Valve: The part of a brass instrument that lets more or less air through in order to play lower or higher tones.

Note to Parents

Awakening Your Children's Interest in Music
- Begin singing with your children from an early age.
- Expose them to a wide variety of quality music in your home.
- Take your children to live music performances.
- If you play an instrument, allow them to play along on their toy instruments.
- Enroll your children in early-childhood rhythm classes.

Choosing an Instrument
- Often children ask to learn an instrument that you have in your home. Make sure the child is physically able to handle it. A nine-year-old, for example, cannot finger a saxophone.
- The child should be intellectually mature enough to follow basic instructions.
- Whatever instrument is chosen, make sure it is the best quality you can afford. Learning on a bad instrument can be discouraging.
- Instead of buying an instrument, you may consider renting one.

Teaching Methods
- Young children enjoy learning in a group.
- The Suzuki method is used for children as young as three years old. It does not teach music reading. Parents are required to learn the instrument with the child.
- The more traditional music teaching, in private or group lessons, requires music reading. Students should be six to seven years old, or old enough to read.

Music Lessons
- A parent should participate in, or be present at, the lesson. This assures that the child practices at home as instructed in class. Young children quickly forget what the music teacher explained. Parental supervision can avoid habits of incorrect posture or ineffective breathing technique.
- If an older child prefers for the parent not to be present during the lesson, then the instructions ought to be briefly discussed with the teacher once the lesson is over.
- Your child's lessons should not be canceled to accommodate your schedule. A lack of your commitment or participation can give negative signals to your child.

Practice Time
- Practice periods should be short but frequent.
- Stay with your child in the same room during practice time.
- It is important for the child to understand that mistakes should be corrected, rather than to play through a melody without stopping. Correcting mistakes brings improvements. This is a great way for a child to understand the concept of learning.
- Your child is bound to make mistakes and experience frustrations. Be encouraging and word critical comments carefully, couched in plenty of positive reinforcement.
- Don't bombard a child with criticism.
- If no regular accomplishments are achieved within a month or two, examine the practice method.
- If you play an instrument, accompany your child and enjoy music making.
- Do not force your child to practice; instead listen to a piece of music together.
- Never use practice as a punishment.

Joining a Junior Orchestra or Band
Once a child reads music and has mastered basic instrument techniques, he or she ought to join a junior orchestra or band. Music making in a group is exciting. It is an incentive to practice because the music has to be studied at home.

Recitals
- Some children perform easily, others are shy.
- If your child refuses to perform, let him or her watch others. With the encouragement and patience of teacher and parent, a child will eventually understand that making mistakes in front of others is okay. Overcoming this shyness can be beneficial later in life.
- Do not have unrealistic expectations.
- Do not compare your child to anyone else.
- Don't expect your child to play for visitors. Most children hate that. They will play on their own if they feel like it.

Behind every successful music student is a committed parent.

Instruments	Instrument Recommended (Earliest Age)	Recommended Starter Instrument	Miscellaneous Information	Size, Weight	Style of Music
WIND *woodwind*	recorder (6)	recorder	inexpensive, easy to learn, fast progress	small, light, portable	classical, folk, popular
	flute (6-7)	recorder (6) piano (3-4)	curved mouthpiece for young students, elaborate breathing and fingering techniques	small, light, portable	band music, classical, folk, jazz, opera, popular
	clarinet (11-12)	recorder (6) piano (3-4)	elaborate breathing and fingering techniques	small, light, portable	band music, blues, classical, jazz, popular
	saxophone (11-12)	recorder (6) piano (3-4)	elaborate breathing and fingering techniques	large, heavy, portable	band music, classical, blues, jazz
	bagpipe (10-12)	recorder (6)	powerful breathing technique and good coordination, expensive, very loud	bulky, heavy, portable	folk
WIND *brass*	trumpet (9)	recorder (6)	sophisticated breathing technique and coordination to produce clean tone, loud but can be muted	small, light, portable	band music, blues, classical, folk, jazz, popular
	sousaphone (14)	trumpet (9)	brass instruments are heavy, fiberglass are lighter; very powerful breathing technique, coordination	bulky, heavy, portable	band music
STRINGS	violin (3-4)	violin	intricate fingering and bowing techniques, tuning	light, portable, available in small sizes	bluegrass, classical, country, folk, jazz, popular
	cello (5-6)	cello	intricate fingering and bowing techniques, tuning	heavy, bulky, portable, available in small sizes	classical, opera, popular
	acoustic guitar (5)	acoustic guitar	intricate fingering technique, tuning	light, bulky, portable	classical, flamenco, folk, jazz, popular
	electric guitar (10)	acoustic guitar (5)	intricate fingering technique, acoustical equipment understanding, tuning	heavy, portable	country, jazz, new age, popular, rock
	harp (7)	piano (3-4)	delicate fingering technique, frequent string replacement and tuning	bulky, heavy, shipping difficult, small teaching harps available	classical, new age, opera, popular
KEYBOARD	piano (3-4)	piano	elaborate fingering technique, fast progress, leg support for small child	stationary	blues, classical, folk, jazz, new age, popular, ragtime
	organ (12)	piano (3-4)	elaborate, hand-foot coordination, practice sessions on location	stationary	classical, rock, sacred
PERCUSSION	drums (5)	drums	sticks and practice pad, snare drum, more drums and cymbals added as progress is made, hand-foot coordination, expensive	bulky, light shipping	classical, jazz, new age, popular, rock
	tambourine (3)	tambourine	early-age rhythm instrument, later used with other percussions	light, small, portable	classical, folk, jazz, opera
	xylophone (9)	drums (5)	small xylophone as an early childhood instrument	small	
			larger xylophone requires wrist technique and good hand coordination	bulky, heavy shipping	classical, jazz, new age, ragtime
VOICE	voice (8)	piano (3-4) recorder (6)	group or choral singing for young children		every style of music
			training for actual vocal production when the vocal cords are more mature